YOU KNOW YOU'RE OLD WHEN...

YOU KNOW YOU'RE OLD WHEN...

A hilarious reminder of how things don't quite happen like they used to!

YOU KNOW YOU'RE OLD WHEN...

Getting lucky means you still have milk left over for your morning coffee.

YOU KNOW YOU'RE OLD WHEN...

You bite into a nut or a lolly and have to go straight to the dentist.

YOU KNOW YOU'RE OLD WHEN...

You yell a lot because you
can't hear yourself speak.

YOU KNOW YOU'RE OLD WHEN...

You can't recall what you had
for breakfast.

YOU KNOW YOU'RE OLD WHEN...

You call everyone 'Darling' because you can't remember their name.

YOU KNOW YOU'RE OLD WHEN...

"Getting a little action"
means you don't need to take
a laxative.

YOU KNOW YOU'RE OLD WHEN...

You look forward to napping
in the afternoon.

YOU KNOW YOU'RE OLD WHEN...

Scrolling to your year date
takes longer than a minute.

YOU KNOW YOU'RE OLD WHEN...

You can't read the writing on your cake because of all the candles.

YOU KNOW YOU'RE OLD WHEN...

The time you used to go out
at night is the time you now
go to bed.

YOU KNOW YOU'RE OLD WHEN...

You walk past the bathroom
and think you might as well
go while you're there.

YOU KNOW YOU'RE OLD WHEN...

You start complaining about
the prices of things.

YOU KNOW YOU'RE OLD WHEN...

You tell a story and everyone leaves the room.

YOU KNOW YOU'RE OLD WHEN...

You are happy you didn't
need to get up to pee.

YOU KNOW YOU'RE OLD WHEN...

You line up your tablets in the morning.

YOU KNOW YOU'RE OLD WHEN...

You walk into a room and can't remember why you went there.

YOU KNOW YOU'RE OLD WHEN...

You leave post-it notes everywhere throughout the house as reminders.

YOU KNOW YOU'RE OLD WHEN...

You email yourself as a reminder to email someone.

YOU KNOW YOU'RE OLD WHEN...

You pull over at the petrol station, run in to buy some milk, then take off without filling your car.

YOU KNOW YOU'RE OLD WHEN...

Everything hurts and what
doesn't hurt doesn't work.

YOU KNOW YOU'RE OLD WHEN...

The gleam in your eyes is from the sun hitting your bifocals.

YOU KNOW YOU'RE OLD WHEN...

It feels like the morning after and you haven't been anywhere.

YOU KNOW YOU'RE OLD WHEN...

Your little black book contains only names that end in M.D.

YOU KNOW YOU'RE OLD WHEN...

Your children begin to look
middle aged.

YOU KNOW YOU'RE OLD WHEN...

You finally reach the top of
the ladder and find it leaning
against the wrong wall.

YOU KNOW YOU'RE OLD WHEN...

Your mind makes contracts
your body can't meet.

YOU KNOW YOU'RE OLD WHEN...

You look forward to a dull evening.

YOU KNOW YOU'RE OLD WHEN...

Your favorite part of the newspaper is "20 Years Ago Today".

YOU KNOW YOU'RE OLD WHEN...

You turn out the lights
for economic rather than
romantic reasons.

YOU KNOW YOU'RE OLD WHEN...

You sit in a rocking chair and can't get it going.

YOU KNOW YOU'RE OLD WHEN...

Your knees buckle, and your belt won't.

YOU KNOW YOU'RE OLD WHEN...

You're 17 around the neck, 42 around the waist, and 95 around the golf course.

YOU KNOW YOU'RE OLD WHEN...

Your back goes out more
than you do.

YOU KNOW YOU'RE OLD WHEN...

Your pacemaker makes the garage doors go up when you see a pretty girl.

YOU KNOW YOU'RE OLD WHEN...

The little old grey-haired lady you helped across the street is your wife.

YOU KNOW YOU'RE OLD WHEN...

You sink your teeth into a
steak, and they stay there.

YOU KNOW YOU'RE OLD WHEN...

You have too much room in the house and not enough in the medicine cabinet.

YOU KNOW YOU'RE OLD WHEN...

All your friends smell like piss.

YOU KNOW YOU'RE OLD WHEN...

Your ears are hairier than your head.

YOU KNOW YOU'RE OLD WHEN...

You name your knees as
either the 'good one' or the
'bad one'.

YOU KNOW YOU'RE OLD WHEN...

You wake up early on days
you can sleep in.

YOU KNOW YOU'RE OLD WHEN...

You've cancelled plans so you could do laundry.

YOU KNOW YOU'RE OLD WHEN...

You grunt when you sit down
and get up.

YOU KNOW YOU'RE OLD WHEN...

You haven't stepped foot in a gym in years.

YOU KNOW YOU'RE OLD WHEN...

Your feet hurt. A lot. And
they smell sometimes too.

YOU KNOW YOU'RE OLD WHEN...

More often than not, you'd rather eat in than out.

YOU KNOW YOU'RE OLD WHEN...

Before you go anywhere,
you consider the parking
situation.

YOU KNOW YOU'RE OLD WHEN...

You hear yourself and you sound just like your mother.

YOU KNOW YOU'RE OLD WHEN...

Sometimes when you stand up fast, you feel yourself losing balance.

YOU KNOW YOU'RE OLD WHEN...

There's nothing left to learn
the hard way.

YOU KNOW YOU'RE OLD WHEN...

You light the candles on your birthday cake, and a group of campers form a circle and start singing "Kumbaya".

YOU KNOW YOU'RE OLD WHEN...

At cafeterias, you complain that the gelatin is too tough.

YOU KNOW YOU'RE OLD WHEN...

You get your exercise acting as a pallbearer for your friends who exercise.

YOU KNOW YOU'RE OLD WHEN...

You know all the answers, but nobody asks you the questions.

YOU KNOW YOU'RE OLD WHEN...

You're asleep, but others
worry that you're dead.

YOU KNOW YOU'RE OLD WHEN...

You quit trying to hold your stomach in, no matter who walks into the room.

YOU KNOW YOU'RE OLD WHEN...

You've grown to appreciate
the refined art of dad humor.

YOU KNOW YOU'RE OLD WHEN...

You are proud of your lawn mower.

YOU KNOW YOU'RE OLD WHEN...

Your best friend is dating
someone half his age...and
isn't breaking any laws.

YOU KNOW YOU'RE OLD WHEN...

Your arms are almost too short to read the newspaper.

YOU KNOW YOU'RE OLD WHEN...

You sing along with the elevator music.

YOU KNOW YOU'RE OLD WHEN...

You would rather go to work
than stay home sick.

YOU KNOW YOU'RE OLD WHEN...

Your children's bedtime is
now later than your own.

YOU KNOW YOU'RE OLD WHEN...

People call at 7 p.m. and ask,
"Did I wake you?"

YOU KNOW YOU'RE OLD WHEN...

The end of your tie doesn't come anywhere near the top of your pants.

YOU KNOW YOU'RE OLD WHEN...

You take a metal detector to the beach.

YOU KNOW YOU'RE OLD WHEN...

You wear black socks with sandals.

YOU KNOW YOU'RE OLD WHEN...

You get into a heated argument about pension plans.

YOU KNOW YOU'RE OLD WHEN...

You have a party and the neighbors don't even realize it.

YOU KNOW YOU'RE OLD WHEN...

When you bend over, you
look for something else to do
while you're down there.

YOU KNOW YOU'RE OLD WHEN...

You try to straighten out the wrinkles in your socks and discover you aren't wearing any.

YOU KNOW YOU'RE OLD WHEN...

At the breakfast table you hear snap, crackle, pop and you're not eating cereal.

YOU KNOW YOU'RE OLD WHEN...

Your back goes out but you stay home.

YOU KNOW YOU'RE OLD WHEN...

You wake up looking like
your driver's licence picture.

YOU KNOW YOU'RE OLD WHEN...

It takes two tries to get up
from the couch.

YOU KNOW YOU'RE OLD WHEN...

Your idea of a night out is
sitting on the patio.

YOU KNOW YOU'RE OLD WHEN...

Happy hour is a nap.

YOU KNOW YOU'RE OLD WHEN...

You're on vacation and your energy runs out before your money does.

YOU KNOW YOU'RE OLD WHEN...

You say something to your kids that your mother said to you and you always hated it.

YOU KNOW YOU'RE OLD WHEN...

All you want for your
birthday is to not be
reminded of your age.

YOU KNOW YOU'RE OLD WHEN...

You step off a curb and look down one more time to make sure the street is still there.

YOU KNOW YOU'RE OLD WHEN...

Your idea of weight lifting is
standing up.

YOU KNOW YOU'RE OLD WHEN...

It takes longer to rest than it did to get tired.

YOU KNOW YOU'RE OLD WHEN...

Your memory is shorter
and your complaining lasts
longer.

YOU KNOW YOU'RE OLD WHEN...

You can injure yourself
in your sleep.

YOU KNOW YOU'RE OLD WHEN...

You barely do anything all day, but still need a nap to continue doing barely anything.

YOU KNOW YOU'RE OLD WHEN...

The pharmacist has become
your new best friend.

YOU KNOW YOU'RE OLD WHEN...

Getting lucky means you found your car in the parking lot.

YOU KNOW YOU'RE OLD WHEN...

The twinkle in your eye is only a reflection from the sun on your bifocals.

YOU KNOW YOU'RE OLD WHEN...

The iron in your blood turns
to lead in your pants.

YOU KNOW YOU'RE OLD WHEN...

It takes twice as long to look half as good.

YOU KNOW YOU'RE OLD WHEN...

Your wardrobe is more about
comfort than anything else.

YOU KNOW YOU'RE OLD WHEN...

Your house catches fire and
the first thing you grab is
your Metamucil.

YOU KNOW YOU'RE OLD WHEN...

You look for your glasses for half an hour and they were on your head the whole time.

YOU KNOW YOU'RE OLD WHEN...

You get two invitations to go out on the same night and you pick the one that gets you home the earliest.

YOU KNOW YOU'RE OLD WHEN...

You drink your one glass
of wine and head home
to go to bed.

YOU KNOW YOU'RE OLD WHEN...

You give up all your bad habits and still don't feel good.

YOU KNOW YOU'RE OLD WHEN...

You get to the check-out line, see how long it is, and decide what you have in your buggy isn't worth the wait.

YOU KNOW YOU'RE OLD WHEN...

You seem to have more patience, but actually it's just that you don't care anymore.

YOU KNOW YOU'RE OLD WHEN...

Rocking in a rocking chair feels like a roller coaster ride.

YOU KNOW YOU'RE OLD WHEN...

You confuse having a clear conscience with a bad memory.

YOU KNOW YOU'RE OLD WHEN...

You finally get your head together and your body starts falling apart.

YOU KNOW YOU'RE OLD WHEN...

You wonder how you could be over the hill when you don't even remember being on top of it.

YOU KNOW YOU'RE OLD WHEN...

You wake up wanting to 'smell the roses' but end up smelling 'the leakage' from the bladder instead.

YOU KNOW YOU'RE OLD WHEN...

Nose hairs are more
abundant than the hairs
on your head.

YOU KNOW YOU'RE OLD WHEN...

You celebrate when your
poo is solid.

YOU KNOW YOU'RE OLD WHEN...

The only thing that gets hard
is your hernia.

YOU KNOW YOU'RE OLD WHEN...

You run out of breath walking DOWN a flight of stairs.

YOU KNOW YOU'RE OLD WHEN...

Your farts smell of Mucilax.

YOU KNOW YOU'RE OLD WHEN...

Everyone laughs when you get angry.

YOU KNOW YOU'RE OLD WHEN...

You get incontinence pants as Christmas presents.

YOU KNOW YOU'RE OLD WHEN...

Restaurants mash your food for you.

YOU KNOW YOU'RE OLD WHEN...

You're the oldest member...
at the bowling club.

YOU KNOW YOU'RE OLD WHEN...

You own a Volvo.

YOU KNOW YOU'RE OLD WHEN...

Your doctor shakes his head
when you see him.

YOU KNOW YOU'RE OLD WHEN...

Children can't believe you
have a driver's licence.

YOU KNOW YOU'RE OLD WHEN...

Your spouse smells like
mothballs.

YOU KNOW YOU'RE OLD WHEN...

You hand the cashier a $5 note to see a movie.

YOU KNOW YOU'RE OLD WHEN...

Food packers offer to carry your purchase to the car at the supermarket…when you've only bought a 1 litre carton of milk.

YOU KNOW YOU'RE OLD WHEN...

You think of going to a 50th birthday party as a 'kiddies' party.

YOU KNOW YOU'RE OLD WHEN...

You laugh and nod enthusiastically at parties – even though you haven't heard a damn word.

YOU KNOW YOU'RE OLD WHEN...

People are amazed that you
still have a parent alive.

YOU KNOW YOU'RE OLD WHEN...

Your teeth sleep at night in a glass.

YOU KNOW YOU'RE OLD WHEN...

Young people ask you for advice.

YOU KNOW YOU'RE OLD WHEN...

Your medical expenses go up 50%.

YOU KNOW YOU'RE OLD WHEN...

Your drugs of preference are now vitamins.

YOU KNOW YOU'RE OLD WHEN...

You develop a knack for
wearing hats.

YOU KNOW YOU'RE OLD WHEN...

Many of your co-workers
were born the same year that
you got your last promotion.

YOU KNOW YOU'RE OLD WHEN...

Your supply of brain cells is finally down to a manageable size.

YOU KNOW YOU'RE OLD WHEN...

Your new easy chair has
more options than your car.

YOU KNOW YOU'RE OLD WHEN...

You can't remember the last time you laid on the floor to watch television.

YOU KNOW YOU'RE OLD WHEN...

Your childhood toys are now
in a museum.

YOU KNOW YOU'RE OLD WHEN...

You read more and remember less.

YOU KNOW YOU'RE OLD WHEN...

You are no longer
'promising'.

YOU KNOW YOU'RE OLD WHEN...

Your investment in health insurance is finally beginning to pay off.

YOU KNOW YOU'RE OLD WHEN...

You don't remember being
absentminded.

YOU KNOW YOU'RE OLD WHEN...

You learn about body parts you've never heard of from constant medical checkups.

YOU KNOW YOU'RE OLD WHEN...

The candles cost more
than the cake.

YOU KNOW YOU'RE OLD WHEN...

The first thing you do at a restaurant is look around...to see where the bathrooms are.

YOU KNOW YOU'RE OLD WHEN...

Injuries from your youth
return with a vengeance.

YOU KNOW YOU'RE OLD WHEN...

The highway patrol sigh or shake their heads but don't give you a ticket.

YOU KNOW YOU'RE OLD WHEN...

No matter how many times
someone repeats themselves,
you still squint and say
"What?".

YOU KNOW YOU'RE OLD WHEN...

You think "hooking up" is a knitting technique.

YOU KNOW YOU'RE OLD WHEN...

You change your underwear after every sneeze.

YOU KNOW YOU'RE OLD WHEN...

An all-nighter means not getting up to pee.

YOU KNOW YOU'RE OLD WHEN...

Your eyes won't get
much worse.

YOU KNOW YOU'RE OLD WHEN...

One of the throw pillows on your bed is a hot water bottle.

YOU KNOW YOU'RE OLD WHEN...

The car that you bought brand new becomes an antique.

YOU KNOW YOU'RE OLD WHEN...

You can go bowling without drinking.

YOU KNOW YOU'RE OLD WHEN...

The waiter asks how you'd like your steak...and you say "pureed".

YOU KNOW YOU'RE OLD WHEN...

You hold all reading material at arms length just to read it.

YOU KNOW YOU'RE OLD WHEN...

You no longer think of speed
limits as a challenge.

YOU KNOW YOU'RE OLD WHEN...

You stop growing at the ends and start growing in the middle.

YOU KNOW YOU'RE OLD WHEN...

You've still got it, but nobody wants to see it.

YOU KNOW YOU'RE OLD WHEN...

Your hot flashes set off the smoke alarm.

YOU KNOW YOU'RE OLD WHEN...

Your insurance company
sends you half a calendar.

First published in 2018 by New Holland Publishers
London • Sydney • Auckland

131-151 Great Titchfield Street, London W1W 5BB, United Kingdom
1/66 Gibbes Street, Chatswood, NSW 2067, Australia
5/39 Woodside Ave, Northcote, Auckland 0627, New Zealand

newhollandpublishers.com

A record of this book is held at the British Library and the National Library
of Australia.

ISBN 9781922256812

Group Managing Director: Fiona Schultz
Designer: Francisco Labra
Printer: Times Printing Malaysia

10 9 8 7 6 5 4 3 2 1

Keep up with New Holland Publishers on Facebook
facebook.com/NewHollandPublishers